SANDHOUR

ROBERT OSTROM

saturnalia books

Distributed by Independent Publishers Group
Chicago

SANDHOUR

ROBERT OSTROM

Saturnalia Books
105 Woodside Rd.
Ardmore, PA 19003
info@saturnaliabooks.com

ISBN: 978-1-947817-10-4
Library of Congress Control Number: 2019937974

Book Design by Robin Vuchnich
Printing by Versa Press

Distributed by:
Independent Publishing Group
814 N. Franklin St.
Chicago, IL 60610
800-888-4741

All my gratitude to Henry Israeli, Christopher Salerno, Robin Vuchnich, and the staff of Saturnalia Books. For encouragement, conversation, and comments, thanks to Pranav Behari, Danielle Blau, Diana Delgado, Hannah Hahn, Tim Hobbs, Thomas Hummel, Timothy Liu, Carey McHugh, Greg Mertz, Addie Palin, Morgan Parker, and Andrew Seguin. To the late Lucie Brock-Broido and Tomaž Šalamun, each of whom continues to guide me through their work and memory. And to Sifu Henry Moy Yee who shows me how to keep doing. Thanks to Greg Mertz for his friendship and the use of his cabin in Maine where this book began to take shape. For their recollections and support, thanks to my family, especially to my sisters, Noelle Swanson, Melissa Ostrom, and Elisabeth Ostrom. For my new family and the grace they fill the life we share, I thank Lisa Jee and Rhea Ostrom.

Table of Contents

PROLOGUE

hope a trailer lack a simple want beginning notion in the gut was real

was not the notion written on the brain a spirit a temper a well of

a power from the well and it does it is as fire to a loving home

WRITTEN ON SKIN

the veins branching
up her legs my mother's
legs girdling roots

left behind the trailer park
for a gusty farmhouse small white
with green trim a garden a yard

grunts and squeals
the seven-fingered
landlord's pig farm
did they mimic
did my sisters

the Cumberlands
through the window
above the kitchen
sink their colors
in autumn she says
light the house

evenings fill rooms with mom
rehearsing choir songs on the upright
and the smell of hamburgers

on the pond across the street
sisters and mother ice skate
should I tell you their names

barely born
into wickedness

winter and the oil
embargo everyone
sleeps in the same bed

the painful
varicose veins
branching up
her legs
from my
mother's legs
the doctor
divines

baptize straightaway
should what have
you occur

in the Southern Baptist
church on Walnut Bottom
Road sisters pray their best
our father who art in heaven

our father is only here
when he hears his name

roaches wander
the floor under her feet
in metal stirrups

the doctor shifts his grip
quotes *Born Again* to dad
mom cries out I am here

new life smells like earth
she has it in her blood
what's to come is inherent
and foaming at the mouth

MY FATHER'S HOUSE HAS MANY ROOMS

truth of this place like sand dunes only
photographs unreliables biases and sister
stories in this memory is myth what the
first frost did to the yard

off the turnpike the bridge to a trail
to a staircase to a lake called trauma
an autumn cold as cold as any cold
and too poor to be warned too
young to know that two hurts
married will only louden the suck in
how they talk familiar solely to kin
what a desert this life she might
think having never been to the
desert

like a son of the church remembers
the church where all memories of the
church are the unfinished church
they've been building in his brain

of radish beet and carrot those taproots
difficult to bring up in pots or relocate
tubers think shame the underground
storage through the year the powersource
countless sweet potatoes he carelessly
planted in her garden then stored up
there still in the colder unfinished attic
above the whole loving family in one bed
roothairs draining the well like fat meat
mean and cursed and coming up on it

is it grass that covers the place where
the kidpool toygrill and picnic table
the whole farmhouse gone is it ryegrass
over where they paced or parked the
wrecked Thunderbird the place where
he stood when his wife quit missing in
the very place she left and does it grow
over things they said the way they said
them and is it now a field no a plot of
grass and how green and pristine
maybe a tree say an aspen but for a
time that plot had a thought stronger
and for a time it had outlines of it does
it still remember

there is no aspen tree in the yard for
the aspen he put there is the aspen he
felled with the axe his grandfather
stole from a friend while cleaning a
barn and the aspen wanted to be on
the first lawn to comfort and
remember his grandfather whom he
loved who was full of gen who once
said these quaking aspen weeds not
good enough for fire and could make a
baseball bat or an axe handle from an
ash branch who knew where the bear
shit in the buckwheat and who
possessed such calm safe that
hummingbirds were known to land on
his hand blue from blood thinners
skin like a teabag cut from work who
one day trashed everything he came to
by impure action so now the axe is the
grandson's he wishes he could use it to
chop down all the trees that forest
what happened set fire to that which
came to him by actions miswired and
hear just once more his grandfather say
a boy after my own heart

but the next house the best house on the
brick road floral couch aloe plant where
notes from spirits in the dirt through an
archway to the foyer where a cedar chest
with winter clothes Hummels on the
mantel red landline upright piano a
painting dad's condoms by the wall
under the bed an arm breaking through
a window a small window sister looking
for her twin

mom's closet her smoking den office railless balcony off the only boy's bedroom where sisters bathed in oil to deepen their skin the impatiens on the porch the windowbox red so hummingbirds would hover painting of a water wagon kids playing in the water a walk-in closet mock fire mom's black plastic cauldron in which geraniums old big white crock where sauerkraut would ferment where kids could hide swingset swing sounds orange blanket Fisher Price kid desk purple flowered wallpaper Jenny the babydoll this house their best house

what's behind his eyes rides the eyes gaum
or by god's foot

bible the family system a house
screened sidedoor basement a
painting of an aunt useful
guidelines from the rulebook had
some dangerous ones sense in the
canning room had his laws in heart
had wrong and wrong was born
again in a closet in the bedroom
artificial warmth from a fire fake
wood over orange film over a light
bulb had a catalpa in the yard was
good in life otherwise in thoughts

in the bedroom woke to whispers and
whisperlaughs the clinking of spoons in
teacups them sipping on the green shag
carpet woke to them gleaming the way
the sky through snow from under snow
as soon as they saw they went

holy water in the hallway newspaper
on sunroom windows in winter a
radiator for warming a root cellar for
fright dirt in her nails tissue paper in
the toes of her shoes on the phone at
the gossip bench in Portuguese
talking to one of her many sisters
who raised each other up in Tauton
their father killed by a wildcat
mother dead on the tenth now her
own lungs wither from years working
the line at the Sanitary Wiping Cloth
Company the rag factory from where
she brought home all the best clothes
grandma in a sleeveless popover
housedress rolls out her upper
dentures with her tongue to frighten
the grandchildren dark-skinned black
curls foul-mouthed a dubious Santa
each Christmas Eve on the Southside
near Swede Hill this house never the

boy's but father's childhood house
filled with a clamor only he his
brother sisters and mother can hear
scent of cookies and linguiça outside
tulips sprouting in the spot where her
husband used to drink and smoke
and sleep under a tree in a lawn chair
his body still swaying from the sea
until his liver gave up and she
covered herself in black and yearning
filled her head each night on a seat
beside a plastic-covered sofa grandma
watches her favorite country dancers
on the television every square foot
and nook chattering behind her
upstairs in her room the infantry pin
hidden in a jewelry box two crossed
rifles on one her first love carved her
nickname the other his last

despite devotion despite assurance
and prospect passage from the best
house despite exorcism by virtue of
reckless by virtue of money the new
house mom's favorite scaldhouse and
no good was it then the split in the
church in the brain the church of safe
from fear and the church of fear

on an avenue named Lakeview with no
view of a lake but past it where one
might run to where locusts so loud she
might think a prop plane or a flock of
hummingbirds too much of anything
even grace as in laying on of the hands
as in a beating to remember a beating
that trails a bloodline this is how a
house haunts a family

want reconciliation spirit without
shame love without temper want the
ceasefire to know they are not locusts
not that squall in the chest want the
man to know the woman the child
who work the insides

early every morning mom walks
down basement stairs for devotions
cigarettes and prayers

here are the church's wide-open arms
the body its nave in its ribs the parish
in pews below the choir like god's
head mother and father rehearse
felicity but the boy is lost again in the
woods behind the parking lot where
outside of his body hymns sound more
like a hum of tree crickets with mud
on his shoes he stands in shoulder-
high underbrush and for a moment
thinks he's in the ground branches
above him are roots until he sees the
steeple point heavenward as if to say
castoff downward thoughts the world
its dirt look up above the swamp the
shame the deeds the thoughts pealing
inside your ears but parents sing
louder his fears

from chicken wire and scrapwood father
builds a cage for the new black bunny as
it grows he adds more cage though the
kids lose interest father adds more still
until before the ice storm the family
hasn't seen the rabbit in half a decade or
more its house a crawlway three-quarters
the length of the garage all that wire
covered in hair and the stink after the
storm its feed piling up father dismantles
the hutch finds the rabbit like a long-lost
toy not even sure it's the same rabbit
fatter than its first cage its coat thinned
patched white

it follows each its rooms inside their
heads like back behind the teeth its
new drapes new floral couch new
sister her beautiful dresses green
turtle-shaped sandbox near the
swallow vein oldest sister in the
finished attic its nooks its tumbled
brick brown bats roosting in the
weep holes broken walkways broken
latches moss like cemetery grass near
the azaleas in the recess behind the
ear father sitting in his chair inches
from the television putting out his
pipe in popcorn kernels stuck below
the jawbone bible verses on the
bedroom walls of their eyes little
sister listening to records up there in
the garret near the crawlspace that's
at the center of the back of the skull
even those who before with their kids
their deeds this house never leaves it
does not follow it leads

though some days on the yellow wall
light skips colors from sister's crystals
swinging in balcony glass and Gretchen
the black lab does not reek the pink
flowered curtains on crescent windows
where her cat said noel and the strong
scent of Irish Spring from the
bathroom after dad's shower his son
drinking cold water from a shaving
cream cap and how the blue carpet in
the pink livingroom is a sky from above
and the porch swing out back can creak
summer they chase bats with tennis
rackets smell tomato leaves or spread
eggshells under mom's lavender by the
flowering dogwood where sisters' prom
pictures all hairspray ruffled sateen

maybe they that built the church or
midway hired new architects maybe
the church was always the church of
fear or maybe it was never even a
church but a house in a town where he
hides from the town a wooden once
farmhouse so old and combustible a
house in a town that grows everyday
more reckless

it was only Saint Christopher says
grandmother who mourning for
decades in black says that man outside
the bedroom holding a baby who rose
slowly until the holes in his feet hard
to say why he rose up past the window
in the violent house his bloody feet it
was only Saint Christopher in black
how pale his skin how outright his
stare there he is see on the dashboard

and clouds could never be clouds
could never be clouds could never be
just clouds for the clouds were the dust
from his feet and he might come in
with the clouds and he was robed in a
cloud and some were baptized in cloud
some were guided by a pillar cloud
above the tabernacle the church and
soon he would sit in a cloud his sickle
in hand and harvest all of this a cloud
could be a witness and he said he
commanded remember whenever the
clouds for a boy looking up at the
clouds just a boy laying on his back in
the grass say on summer break and
thinking and listening to hear a voice
from the cloud say this is my son this
my son and never a cloud could be just
a kid cloud or on any ordinary day

saint take to your heels saint tooth hurt
mother of Salems mother of devotion in
the laundry room servant to the king in
the moss colored kitchen saint videogame
sounds from the basement the devil to
god light as a hummingbird around the
neck of a grandmother heavy as upheaval
on the shoulders of a boy saint coming for
to carry across rivers saint doghead saint
go away

how to assemble shame how to lose
faith where to go to find a compass
where the beaver dam in the woods
where a bird falls dead at feet where
to race bullfrogs where sand dunes
where to climb the edge of a dune a
giant anthill where the red ants cover
arms where to learn to plait rope
where slapped by familiar hands
where humiliated where runaway
where a found swimming hole and
where in a spillway and felt it leaving
the body and how he prayed it back
and how it hurt the body and was it
even what was prayed for how when
older he sat drinking cheap beer with
other kids in this same woods and
knew by his eye every warren trail the
surging buzz of insects and a faraway
train and when drunk how he told no
one of the time he spilled gasoline
that set fire to the girl and how every
fire is the same fire and how he knew
at least three people on fire

important to remember is melting to
glass important to fix to hold to ruin
the stitch like a blanket made of sand or
how like grasping to sandbanks a sand
rope sand memory sand thoughts sand
bodies sand bible sand house

in the heat of a field near the side of
a road the low incessant clack and
hum of grasshoppers and cicadas
with milkweed sap on skin where the
sting in the web of fingers his love is
more noise than fever

before bed he'll forgive touch the
four corners of the room touch all
sides of the bed he'll forgive two at
once touch two sides at once with the
back of the hands the windows touch
them with the forehead kiss the
pictures all four sides of the frame
touch his face kiss his face touch the
door open the door close the door
touch the door with knuckles lay
down say your prayers get up touch
the mirror pray he'll forgive the
fingertips with the back of the hands
at the same time the TV screen with
palms with all the fingers and the
palms feel static then the cool and
cautiously pull both lightstrings
above the bed and pray and pray and
pray now to the floor the rough and
dirty green and knees and pray for
sleep and to bed now for the fears

OF JOINTS AND MARROW

like a son I will do for you all you
ask at night where you go I will
be leftover for anyone in whose
eyes find favor buried or picked
up I will not be remembered I
will stay even if night deal with
me be it ever so severely

when there is no longer any
blood to take away take away
unbelief

for troubles without number
surround me I dwell as a
stranger as all my fathers were
whoever follows me never walks
how faint the whisper hear it
claps its hands in derision and
hisses me out of place

if you call will you teach me
where I have been wrong quiet
me so to hear it the penalty of
deliverance from houses from
parents hot-tempered from
wealth from prudent from
medicine had I solved my riddle
I would not have inherited a
thousand jawbone words

all the things I do I carry you
sustain you you are a way out
look at you coming with clouds
and every eye because I am
yourselves will mourn because
of

in skin of or I will be

if only there were someone
between us to lay a hand upon
us both and without fear it was
not our father but with us with
all of us who in the shelter of
our tongues

a champion named pour out
your hearts

the deep says he is not me the
lord says he is not with me

because haunts of violence confess
to each take captive every thought
make obedient and know while
you were still on earth as it is
under the field under the fig
setting a plumb line all deserted
and fled into my room stay here
and keep watch pray the line
which can save me do not let my
hand know close the door renew
within thought every harmful
word

now these three remain sacrifice
condemn and remember but the
greatest of these is remember

your outstretched neck waters
my tongue the house the harp
and arrows the things you have
promised promise and stain and
promise alone meat is better in
the desert why did I ever

suffer these things day after day
in the place where I thief and
joy fall and give up

forgive for they know my sins

have overtaken and I cannot see

how much more shall I be made
drunk in the grass who is but grass

because you refused me at the
door I spend my voice far from
you because you eat truth I will
not be saved

I will stay in the desert and live
in sin for grace the desire for
has mastery over me

I slept but my head was awake
he was knocking drenched
with dew the wolf the gazelle
the doe the lamb they charge
the field it yielded only bad
fruit I open my lips I swallow
my keep my speak what is I
live with what is robbery what
is inequity the sea that pride of
drunkards he swallows it I slept
but my head was awake the law
was knocking

then turned away from him a
heart field hangs neither sleep
nor overwhelmed and fled is
sorrow

and on the ground appeared again
they those who left who heard
them body do everything left you
unfinished to the church go down
to again to

DROWNING DOESN'T LOOK LIKE DROWNING

through our neighborhood
then another father
he brought me toward
the rented plot my feet
blistering father hell-bent
I tried to keep up I felt
a wisp of laughter followed
me at times boredom made
the ache truer and some
counsel came from
rain-scented trees they
said go back still something
about walking with him
felt almost like being seen

halfway I picked up
a stick as we crossed
the street and down
the sidewalk I dragged
it along the cemetery
fence which seemed to
quicken his pace when
we reached the end
of the flat I threw
the stick as far as I
could my father flinched
scolded me I was
parched he was afraid
my father he never drank
imagination not guilt
enough to make him drunk
and we drank cold water
from a graveyard spigot

someday the cemetery
would extend into the land
where we grew tomatoes
cabbage and all the vegetables
mother would can for winter
but before that on a dirt mound
I stood in the cool of his shadow

he talked of roses
the size of trees
as he raked the soil
he found a satchel
of old money
my father stood
taller than most men
I hung my hopes
there against
his infallible back
or on his arms I hung
them like a bear bag
strung to a branch
in either case
I hung my hopes
too low the moths
laid eggs in the winter
clothes I was wearing
when they asked how
I got these bruises

in his stare the war
in his evening hands
fingers that would
bend pennies I should
have known his life
couldn't bear the weight
of his own acts

maybe it was never his angle
maybe he didn't have the stomach
for it though the way he'd
tighten a knot look at me and spit
in the dirt he didn't strike me
my father's gaze seldom
directed at his intention

once I fell into a river
once trapped under the raft
I rolled in a sleeping bag
slipped between the bed
and wall I never came out

he wasn't the one
who taught me how
to build an altar
he wasn't an altar
builder but it was
a kind of sacrifice

know I was hiding
in the cupboard

as everything was taken
from me except my life

I like to pretend

my daughter's name
means exempt

I wish you
such relief

when all you fear

is at last here

when we returned
home I mistook
his black hair for
cracks in the sink

THE CHILDREN'S TEETH SET ON EDGE

to be poorly dressed in another's

dread to study train practice to be just

like them is to rehearse for a play

about a family to be stalked by those

not curbed by death though buried

generation after generation of

back pain nail biting fear of water

the symptoms are symbols

erection of walls for example

bulwarks parapets hedges are distrust

fear of intimacy claustrophobia

anxiety a near-drowning at a pool party

poor eyesight body-hatred laziness at work

to live as secrets hidden behind a bureau

obsession over inadequacies

familiar is anger and antipathy

back pain nail biting headaches

judgmental disapproving impostor

syndrome student loans credit card debt

diarrhea self-hatred disgust in relationships

a near drowning in a river

to live as the agony in his eyes

yes lord you know sometimes to the ground

slicing along new skin of an old wound

glory peeling it open and watching

hallelujah his face its anguish is a story

of return overly tired most of the time

inability to sleep at night

visions in the dark for example

sexual anxiety aversion to authority

trepidation when leaving the house

dislike of doctors alcoholism

fear of god fear especially of unforgivable

offence inability to resist blasphemy

before bed children as mirrors

children as audience for instance

nightmares of humiliation love us

they say or we will come at you wilder

daydreams of avenging humiliation

father jokingly crooning all the time nobody

knows the trouble I've seen nobody knows

but Jesus while somewhere in the deep rich earth

of his brain his drunk father beats his mother

with an iron desire for adulation distrust

of adulation drug addiction always

chiding like what am I about

comfort in canning cooking

and dishes stuffed cabbage and peppers

golden jubilees when a favorite place

in this world was the base of a tree

aloneness with a view

of the lake desire for solitude

solitude then loneliness

ambivalence regarding narrative

image fixation such as a feather

in a dictionary waiting too much

for the right skin

guilt oodles of it

for example dad's wishplans

lack of safety

attraction to meanness

grandmother's trauma like an heirloom

when her son husband

and daughters open the garage

find her in the car how a cage

changes its animal

becomes a long-felt absence as if

born with a feeling of chasing

various rituals before bed

urge to control those nearest

stomach pain silliness as concealment

selfishness high blood sugar overweight

dry skin destructive needs

the way a cut sapling elaborates the wound

neglect fear of infidelity

infidelity ire toward rational choices

and the economy of emotion

a near drowning then a rescue

the one who keeps watch is the one who

neglects is the one who saves

father singing please release me let me

go haunts in every joint

a hole in the fence is escape

then another stronger fence

emerges in the near distance

back pain headaches acid reflux

attaching emotion to junk hoarding

thereof obsessive compulsions like

shoes in line equilibrium with touch

everything in its place

desire to be free of it in harmony

mother and father sing dream

dream dream dream dream

the equity of blame

to want it in my arms

like unpacking luggage like organizing

all their charms to be in love with

whenever I want to all I have do

is look forward to one more fire

ON EARTH AS IT IS

in the middle of my life I went back

the lawn waterlogged as always

trudged in from the dirt

road down the ditch through

tillage and into pines a familiar

scratch of high grass catchweed

clawing legs I rounded the garden

toward the pond away from the house

then south back into trees

past the empty wood duck nest

until I reached his deer stand

fifteen feet up the ladder

of two-by-fours nailed to the trunk

climbed to get a better view

and looking back saw my mother

on the near-finished porch the sheepdog

beside her herding hummingbirds

my sister walking out of the barn

eggs in her shirt my sister riding

the lawn tractor around the apple

tree my sister fishing from the barrel

dock and between her and the house

he is teaching me how to set brick

along the flower garden on a stump

a barn nail driven through a catfish

he skins and guts it right there

I see its eyes searching

I see me carrying the bones still

writhing to the compost heap

fern and tinder fungus the sulfur

scent sucking sound of a boot in a gully

of meltwater and there that one spot

in the woods a circular clearing

surrounded by hemlocks when the sun

was right a hallowed place my secret

where a ring of light as if god set down

his crown and didn't notice me small

thing standing in the middle I'd pray mud

tracks lead back to the coop where from

the Massey tractor's treads peels of earth

before he dug the pond I send an arrow

from the edge of the woods into the family

reunion the whole tribe scatters except

for a crippled aunt in her electric wheelchair

and near her the one they said possessed

a faith so firm she could see her own angel

then I'm in college and we're running

jumping to catch pheasants that escaped

there I'm a boy again returning from

a drive on the butterfly hills against the barn

wall he takes a hammer to the willful

rooster from the stand I turned to look

farther into the woods saw myself firing

his shotgun smoking a cigarette

after Thanksgiving dinner felling aspens

growing into the lawn looked down

and saw myself fucking my girlfriend

beside a tree then some twenty years

back lost in the cornfield east past

the woods on top of the hill and even

back when I was younger holding a bunny

while he built the split-rail fence watched

grownups throw lawn darts send me out

to the old pickup Leer under which lumber

and under that crawlers for bluegills

tadpoles on the shore from the paddle

boat a brace of reclusive Israeli carp

colossal and auburn older than my

sister who pulls at the fishhook inside

her thumb not knowing the way

to free a hook is to push it through

while out in the garden he sets mattress

springs to separate seeds I saw us

roast apples and hotdogs for dinner

that night we camp near the wood's edge

but far enough from houselights

here there is no place to sleep safe

from snakes fingers blueberry-stained

the afternoon katydids splitting

a Cortland with his bare hands

he offers me half but I'm nowhere

this perch now over thirty years old

the wood cracks the tree barely stands

under my weight my view dims

is this what the barn swallow saw

when it disappeared into the pond

was what great grandmother thought

as she looked out over it tapping

her nails to a tune she nearly forgot

and a memory she wished she had

lost in mud like quicksand up to her

ankles her slippers coming off in it to say

the earth sucks you in what if the branch

comes down on your tent while you sleep

what is kin what is inheritance

if not we are gone but the same

birds come back how do you parcel

a life in this patch of landscape

are the units the scream the touch

the sigh and the laugh what if a person

is a family what if the Ford Escort

is still in the driveway the arrow

is still in the air the last of sunlight

perpetually dims as a boy tries to pull

down cornstalks to get some sense

of where he is and there on the deck

grandma shoots the snapping

turtle at a far piece hear

its report silence the woods

the forest holds its breath until

a red-winged blackbird responds

and the distance erupts into song

the last time I saw him before

I reached the house I stopped

to watch a great horned owl at

roost in one of his tall pines I used

to have this compulsion to turn

everything into symbol but by

then I resisted it and now I wish

I hadn't all these things that were

outside the body mud smells

the goldfinch insects screeching

upstairs lemon meringue pie

a wet dog sisters giggling a sudden

hiss then snap in the fire they all live

in here now dyed-in-the-wool

while behind them moves something

reptile someone is taking wire cutters

to the fishhook inside a thumb and even

though they put him down twenty

years ago the sheepdog is still in the grass

trying to shepherd his own shadow

THIS HOUSE AFFIRMS A RESOLUTION

one dreams of a house

that contains all others

a Tudor with a pool

a deck a large kitchen through

which a garden tall hardwoods

then mountains one dreams

of a finished basement with

a canning room laundry machine

a place for devotion one dreams

that in the house that contains

all other houses is the childhood

bedroom and there one finds all

the childhood things on the green

shag carpet a Speak & Spell

beside the yellow plastic briefcase

and inside a diary old batteries

a pocket knife shotgun shells

the room is cluttered with memory

a magnet covered in rusty paperclips

there is the boat-building book

The Spell of the Yukon a sink

in the closet there a tiny jar of Maine

sand the room smells acrid

but the scent is familiar calming

all over the floor are photographs

and toys and on the wall are cutouts

from magazines and bible verses

the word temporary written out

defined and taped above

the mirror and suddenly

one remembers his dog

is waiting in the car it's time to go

dogs should not be left in cars

but there are so many treasures

of childhood here and only

a few more minutes when from under

a pile of small clothes that smell like

the best house one sees a rabbit the rabbit

is dirty but adorable and then one notices

maggots on the floor and this is how

the rabbit has survived by eating the maggots

has it been here all this time

where did it come from and one knows

he needs to leave the dog

is in the car what if the dog can't breathe

it's time to go his father with arms

crossed is angry one is not welcome

in this house he looks up from the floor

and out the window Saint Christopher

is not there mother does not live there

and all the while the rabbit nuzzles and plays

he knows if his father finds the maggots

he'll throw away all the treasures

and so one sprays the room

with Lysol a whole bottle of Lysol

and leaves the house that contains

all the other houses and outside

in his father's old SUV his dog waits

so patiently one worries for a second

that he is dead but he's okay the dog

is clean and well cared-for it behaves

and when one wakes up he would like

to think himself a good person but inside

he knows the dream is the always feeling

the animals his parents his little sister all

his old things a procession like a long

heavy rope tied to his brain they hang

counterweights as if from a deep well

below calling to him pull us pull us up

MEANS FOR DELIVERANCE

x

MEANS FOR DELIVERANCE

115

here is the knife
take captive every
thought deed
deal with severely

next time you
visit I'd like
to tell you
about farmhands
who in silos
slip into
the grain
and suffocate
jaws broke open
in final awe

did you bleed for me
and did my face did you
pay my debts would you
vote for me did
you shut grace in

you be shepherd
I'll be rebuilt joyful
noise in a field
in which I stray

in Maine the saltmeadow
a close-up of a horse's crest

make me lie
down in
the meadow
so I can
woolgather
and witness

inside the house
I burn my
worry is
a hummingbird
caught in a
spider web

because in shame I found
a well sounds homespun
called me down twenty
feet or so the well it lived
with me and I would edge
into my place body
my daily bread until I saw
what I drank was standing
water and hatred was bread
let this be the grout I shovel

we are
all root
and choices
we bear
a weight
like Sarah
stand between
memory and
the whole story

pull open
a family
step into
the abysslight
find a compass
we'll settle
accounts stretch
our hands
be finished with

you be unearthed
tubers I'll be a day
without ritual

CONTROLLED BURN

the resin-rich heartwood
is firm and difficult
to cut so close
to the ground
I use the blunt side
of the double bit
I splinter the stump
and chop at
taproots I harvest
joints where tree
limbs meet they call
this fatwood richlighter
prized as kindling
and its smoke
first-rate repellent

in the early
morning fog
on Smedley Road
a dirt road
in the western
Pennsylvania woods
my grandmother
rushing
braked for a deer
a young
deer with small
velvet antlers she
said it wouldn't
leave was looking

at her she said
hey you
get out of my way
but it stood
its ground

having rehung
his axe having
driven the wedge
he had driven
into the eye
having sharpened
with the mill bastard
file then spitting
on the bevel
and with a whetstone
straightening the burr
sanding the handle
finishing with
linseed oil
combustible
he might've said
as the compost pile
where catfish molt
having let it soak
feeling its heft
I realize
it never needed
to be rehandled
his job was done

better I take the rag
to the fire pit
and watch it burn
if you're going
to do something
I hear him say you
may as well
do it right

when she finally
arrived at the hospice
home the nurse looked
at my grandmother
Heidi she said
you just missed him
on the phone
later that day
I told her the deer
on the road
it must've been
Granddad she paused
and said he would
have been upset
coming back
a spike buck
she said
he would've wanted
an eight-point rack

I build a fire
in the cast
iron hearth
and the logs
are of the wood
my grandfather
split from trees
that were
saplings when
I was a boy

he could light a match
with the strike of an axe
I like to think
he had sap
on his arms
the morning he died
the nurses
I imagine
mistook black
walnut stains
on his hands
for bruises
that day
when they burned
his body
the funeral home
smelled like pine

sometimes I feel
like a catalpa
branch growing
from an ash tree
what a wilderness
this life

Also from Robert Ostrom:

The Youngest Butcher in Illinois

Ritual and Bit

Sandhour was printed using the font Adobe Garamonde.

www.saturnaliabooks.org